so we have been given time   or

T0125098

SO WE HAVE BEEN GIVEN TIME OR

SAWAKO NAKAYASU

verse press amherst, massachusetts

Published by Verse Press

Library of Congress Cataloging-in-Publication Data
    Nakayasu, Sawako, 1975–
        So we have been given time or / Sawako Nakayasu. — 1st ed.
        p. cm.
    ISBN 0-9746353-0-8
    I. Title.
    PS3614.A575S6 2004

                                                    2004004090

Available to the trade through Consortium Book Sales
and Distribution, 1045 Westgate Drive, St. Paul, MN 55114

Printed in the United States of America

9 8 7 6 5 4 3 2

so we have been given time   or

DIRECTIONS: take 95 south to 195 east, exit gano st.
don't park.

TIME: within the frame.
too late for changes in the master plan.
enormous changes at which minute.
go back for more

CHARACTER: a new degenerate.
confessional rock star.
at dinner tells a bad joke about silence, thank you.
next

DIRECTIONS: amtrak.
south.
south.
sentimental thoughts on a train, by the window, with a
    paper cup, an old cup of tea.
cup as focus or locus, as if it starts with

TIME: shortened by ice floes departing downriver.
moreshortened by clouds reflecting samely samely on such

PLACE: directions.

DIRECTIONS: get on the subway, any system.
buy a bag, get sneaky about it.
ask the right questions to the unsuspecting.
open an unmarked door in the

DIRECTIONS: more crying.
               trans-atlantic

CHARACTER: person with both eyes closed in heathrow airport.

DIRECTIONS: a phone number has x as a digit.
               begin to suffer.
               run alongside, parallel to time as if this is done all the time.
               stay in airport for pragmatic or hugely contentious reasons.
               read as little as possible into the voice on the phone.

CHARACTER: the arrived and the recalcitrant.

DIRECTIONS: stub.
               stun gun aimed at

TIME: encapsulates itself or is wrapped, flea-bomb or christo.
dead-ring circus.
laugh out loud for the last

TIME: given.
prove.
innocuous to the end but stunned all the same

CHARACTER: stunning.
in an orange bar.
change of heart to be determined the following year.
kissing buttress held up by

TIME: out for a breath of freezing.
glacial, escaping, wrought about.
fevered with resentient beings.

TIME: one minute remaining

TIME: on a residual penalty

TIME: give it up for an interlude.
for a personal interview.
impersonal sick day.
personal reasons for breaking up every

TIME: one standard

TIME: one minute plus one continent plus one long car ride

TIME: stilled.
                    not enough

TIME: slowed by layer upon layer of clothing and excess.
                    accessories as condiment.
                    scarves, a length of

TIME: given.
                    running.
                    in appropriate.
                    eating someone else's

TIME: conspired to the point of friendly distortion.
                    friendly distortion.

VARIATION: father, as in oh.

PLACE: electronic.

DIRECTIONS: perpetual east, past every torso.
                    field, a question.
                    field every physicality.

DIRECTIONS: don't say anything or don't say something.
                    ask, away.
                    keep mouth full of time.
                    take it or eat it.
                    to go.
                    a heart full of

DIRECTIONS: fill the blank heart with blanks.
                        shot through the night.
                        in a foreign bar.
                        after eating.
                        after day, its false safety.

CHARACTER: meet you at such or which place.
                        everyone not this

CHARACTER: family.

CHARACTER: history.

CHARACTER: years, a large percentage.

MEASURE: all in the same season, but spanning many years and tears
of foolish sincere youth and promise and no bells just beings
and theres and a lost token or touch, resting on the shoulders
of a couple of tenuous

CHARACTERS: here unnamed but tender nonetheless and resting
                        as usual on the fragmentary exchange of

CHARACTER: in relation to an international picket fence.
                        brimming with

DIRECTIONS: gotiate.
                        golightly.
                        findings.
                        from any angle.

DIRECTIONS: continue, or
make more tea.
enter one more

CHARACTER: countless.
immeasurable.
at great lengths.
what does this mile mean.
what if to mean is not to know.
what kind of knowing could now matter.

DIRECTIONS: take train from one night into the next.
against all willing parties.
the trouble with train station employees who would help
if only.

VARIATION: getting off.

VARIATION: not getting off like that

CHARACTER: complected and turning lovely.
at the off-chance.
turning complected.

PLACE: still towarding on.
to ward off

DIRECTIONS: ignore the overhead exclamation.
interpret silently, personally.
silence to be stowed away.
acknowledge without response.

DIRECTIONS: how long to continue is a matter of

DIRECTIONS: are being given still.

CHARACTER: no one of good would get off like this.
turns dark and lovely.
with mildly contentious reason.
falls into the wrong

HANDS: together in unsettlement

HANDS: cathedrals everywhere

HANDS: across a passing object.

PLACE: framed in a false photograph.
framed in a written note.
given notes.
undelivered unnoticed

SOUND: phone call from the other side.
long.

SOUND: english everywhere.

SOUND: not english everywhere.

SET: balcony outside a bus.
same set of stoppage.
snow.

snow.

more snow.

less.

SET: get out

DIRECTIONS: lean against or away from joy.
                a considerate and considerably large mogul.

CHARACTERS: overaged intellectuals behind an unmarked door.
                someone's need to shave.
                walking uphill in a lovely.
                hold baggage in a lovely.
                sandwiches are a lovely

PLACE: tenuous aim at place.

PAUSE: take all of it for a momentary walk in the park.

TIME: go.
                fatten.
                bus.
                train.
                go.
                car.
                load.
                load.
                a loaded

SOUND: tenuously in french.

PAUSE: as never having happened.

SOUND: a mouth full of food.
             inverted umbrella.
             kindness of old friends.
             kindness of old people.
             getting wet at the wrong time.
             drinking in.
             a long

SOUND: of thirst.
             long hunger.
             rolling.
             growl.
             kindness of men.
             beer at the wrong nation.
             beer at the right nation.
             timing full of beer.

CHARACTER: still.
             and still.
             and still.
             teasing out the lovely.
             looking up the lovely.
             mucking up potential lovely

DIRECTIONS: toward more tenuosity.

TIME: slowing.
             increasingly angular.

slowing.
more viscous.

vicarious.
vicious.

quiet.
more viscous

DIRECTION: which train.
which trust.
every vehicle a person.
every person a vehicle.
residual vehemence.

DIRECTION: away.
apostrophe.
cross-road.
offstage.
do nothing with immediacy.
exit from a lack of

SETTING: flimsy joy.
forthcoming, to be detained.

PLOT: of coastal illness.
a sweeping malaise.
stranger grandma.

CHARACTER: female or persuaded.

DIRECTIONS: 5 south.

CHARACTER: pervasive.

DIRECTIONS: border.

OFFSTAGE: false balcony.
false alas balcony.
false false illusive balcony.

CHARACTER: on stage.
a lack, effort.

THEME: present day.
against all struggle for

IRONY: cathedrals everywhere.

DIRECTION: mexico.

TIME: wrap it up.

TIME: breaking.

TIME: tied up.
bound.
affixt.
fettery.
up.
pinioned.
pressive.

PRESSURE: san ysidro crossing.

PLACE: ready-made street.

TIME: catered.
breaking everywhere.

COSTUME: shedding.
shedding light.
shedding weight.
what changes.

CONSUME: daylight.
time.

MAKE: not good time.

PLACE: approaching tendency.
that face.
that voice.
that situation.
have been there before.
have not have not.

RESOLUTION: unsolicited

CLIMAX: a year ago

LEADING: here and here.
all heres on deck.

SPOKEN: all hail.

SAILS: an interlude of water.

CONTINUOUS: cathedrals everywhere.

CHARACTERS: no practicing.
              practicing to be a spectator.
              practicing the cross.
              crossing the bend.
              bending a green card.
              holding on, mere innocence of

CHARACTERS: keep.
              kept.
              keep.
              uncalled for.
              dropping.

DROPPING: people.
              a grounded folk.
              the ground in the fork.
              fork to mouth.
              to ear.

PHONE: call.
              call from a dark.
              call from a long white patrol.
              and yet and yet a noplace of origin.
              gives rise to the usual propensity games.

that we thought we thought were too old to still be playing.
still.

LANGUAGE: topography of emotional gunned forth and slight outbursts.
thirdhand transversal.
striangulation.

REGULATED: by geographical prejudice.
barred like a dog.

PLOT: tijuana consistency.

PLACE: her sense of we've been this way before.
we've been this way before.
we've been had this way before.
having had children and where.

PLACE: breaking it up.

TIME: breaking it up.

CONFLICT: blanking it up.
filling in blank forms.

CONFLICT: blanking on memorized eye chart.

CONFLICT: blanks.
blanket.

BLANKLY: the whites of.
                blinkings.
                blinking to get heard.
                blinking to cross.
                linked to a long history of lines, many thicknesses.
                thickness.
                drawn out

MOMENTS: conclusions everywhere.

PLOT: fishing for

CHARACTERS: who.

CHARACTERS: subject.

CHARACTERS: subject to

PLOT: action as discovered on the line.
                gunning for.
                gunning forth.
                stun gun aimed this time at

PLOT: split.
                 then.

CHARACTERS: make a long sound.
                 the kindest attendant at the lastest hour.
                 with no language at all.
                 or practical

PLOT: a letter.
                 lengthened wait.
                 exchange.
                 handed over all personals.
                 letter and person.
                 a secret car.
                 sheets.
                 illness.
                 sleep.
                 approaching the tenuous land with a breath of fresh.
                 sleep its length through.
                 a woman turns kind.
                 borders act with temporary gentle.
                 with gentle tenuous.
                 directed toward the familiar foreign.
                 tenuous yet owned unapologetically.
                 tenuous yet distant from actual source.
                 tenuous lovely to glance from a distance.
                 tenuous lovely beaming away or rolling past.
                 tenuous on its own terms.
                 tenuous on its own turfed country.

tenuous because and acceptingly and free to be on its
own tenuous lovely ground.
tenuous grounding itself instantly solidly as a matter of
factual discourse or resolution.
tenuous and over or over it or over itself as an
acceptance as an acknowledgement.
tenuous and even perhaps fake or unreasonable yet
coming into its tenuously owned term.
tenuous its turn and turning.
tenuous because every character affected.
tenuous and attaining towards.
tenuous as light would have its way with.
tenuous you, might dare say a place.
tenuous or a name.
tenuous or an act of nebulous yet sincere

TENUITY: all of the below.

BELOW: in the light of many many years accrued.

YEARS: 1988–2000.

1993:   declaration.

1994:   proof.

1995:   phased solid and clear but not ice.
              under influence of.
              under blue.
              under neatly.
              telephone.

TELEPHONE: inadequacy begins its head.
              negotiations on everyone's dime.
              pointing to an obviously obscure.

DIRECTION: this, in such obvious obscure

DIRECTION: this, in the tender present from above.
              obviously obscure gift from above

DIRECTION: make a series of choices.
              an old chaos or home.
              sameness of street.
              just after a big birthday.
              birthday loaded with.
              clarity or joy.
              fast breath of

LANGUAGE: diminutive name or clarity.
              familiar name or truth.
              and truth.

GAME: checking the right box.
              recapturing the flag.
              a game of story.
              a marionette.

PLOT: safe to eat.
              for most intents and persons.

TIME: shared.

PLOT: return to as opposed to remember.

DECLARED: 199x the year of

PLOT: memory wins out.

DECLARED: first born yang-ish.

PLOT: birthday cake holds its ground after many too many parties.

CAKE: as sugared tenuous example.
                as necessary edible element.
                as easy as any other baked good, a whole lineup of mothers
                with their sleeves rolled up, revealing muscles, definition,
                tension, not as a result of baking, but for some given flighty
                moment using cake as

RESISTANCE: to tyranny.

SKIP: old news.
              conceptual children.
              extenuous present stance.

TIME: discontinued

TIME: standard chinese

TIME: tenuous to the end.

EAT: safely.
              other dangers called

REALITY: of old friend.
             same child, larger version.
             wasted arms.
             new neighbor.
             more dangers called

CHILDREN: being in love with.
             desire to protect.
             owning a couple.

SET: a familiar clutter.
             bustle of young laughter hung up on the walls.
             falls into place which is to say face or floor or recovery
                 time not included.
             whose face to save

TIME: intent from the get-go and to the end, and asking for it.

TIME: enough to get sick.
             enough to get sick from a big holiday.
             enough to watch more than sufficient numbers of lug-
             gage thrown from more than sufficient numbers of flights
             with more than sufficient love in the form of this

SONG: bossed in from downstairs

SONG: she'll be coming.
             play the manon for the kid.
             when she comes.
             play the kid for the mom.

play mom and sing.
the little boat.
the dusty boat.
try not to get worried.

TIME: enough to get better.
in the countryside.
more than sufficient to eat.
to leave it as such.
matter of consumption.

BACK: in the city.
on the floor.
when the neighbor picks up a bar on the way home from

NOT WORK: what sculpting.
what writing.
what artists wouldn't and would do.
listen to what someone has said from afield, drifting,
    edged and trying.
to enact what with a vengeance.
to give what with a vengeance.
to show up with a vengeance.
many many elsewheres and others.

PROOF: by photography.
by absence.

DEMENTINGS: this doesn't qualify.

QUALIFICATIONS: hold true in specified light.
                  hold truth in a handbag.
                  hold two hands in one pocket.
                  hold any two hands together in any given
                      circumstance such as

CATHEDRALS: everywhere.

SPECIFICATIONS: standard human operational temperature.
                  built-in cooling system.
                  a

LIGHT: which may need to take place in the form of con-
         nection, which may need to take place in the form of
         touch, which may need to take place in the form of
         skin, which may need to take place in the form of
         someone shipped in from elsewhere, which may
         need to take place on the horizontal, which may need
         to take everyone back to the beginning of the story,
         which may need to take more time, or more story, or
         more places than this, which may need to take place
         in the form of several or multiple people getting to-
         gether and conspiring as to light or no light and what
         kind of light and how much intensity is ours for the
         controlling and how much light is ours for the keep-
         ing or having or holding touching all the whiling dol-
         ing out and tending the keep, last keep of light trip-
         ping availability from this end, that end, this end, that
         end of the continuum of this particular human con-
         viction and yes, the problem with it all, let us perhaps
         toss out that convicted light and see what happens.

WHAT HAPPENS: not a pleasant word.
                request for money.
                and copies of photographs.
                proof of nonexistence.
                churches lose their meaning.
                churches lose their irony.
                churches lose to more exotic architectures such as a
                    party.
                cathedrals lose their money.
                but children keep track

LIGHT: from a child.
                unspecific heat.

WHAT HAPPENS: many many years ago a spanish painter wrote some
                poems that managed to keep, get kept, dug up,
                dredged up in a bar on a little street teeming with flies
                and so this is really happening.
                architecture of a party.
                flamenco trilling loudrageous, this wall that wall
                    with this-such proximity.
                bustle of poetry.
                linger of poetry, or its turned generation.
                a civilized crowd.
                enter

BALCONY: cathedrals everywhere.

EVERYWHERE: angles in the architect's eye pointing upwards.
                asking what the fact would do.
                tripped to the first stool.

narrowed back and slip into morning, squared.
to the squared.

TRIP: no longer a trip.
root of all.
squared mind, quirreling away at the nearest human
traffic light.

TRIP: on it again.
an interruption of water.

TRIP: stay on it.
stay civilized.

RIP: into a wink.
as in, tear, as in, a, way, from, that, which, is, not, and,
otherwise,

BETTER LEFT: to older vices.
stop turning right.

AS IF: right.
right.
made it two blocks away from home.
on a familiar vice.
unflagging or immediate conviction of all involved
characters.

DIRECTIONS: angle self towards a free kick.
buy no more fish.
buy fish with its water.

watch them die.
be culturally sensitive. toilets are for shit.
bury them in the plants.
collect tadpoles in a ruinous garden.
watch them get eaten.
be naturally sensitive. death of a fellow fish.

CHARACTERS: this man is mad.

CHARACTERS: this woman is sad.

CHARACTERS: this man this woman in the form of a collision in a narrow
stairwell narrower than his belly her ass in the form of
what is this good for nothing to do with nothing to do with
the force of collision but you, friend, get out of this place
is toxic hazardous to the good upkeeping of hands, feet,
fish, life, hence the pole.

TIME: a tad of love. a smatter of course.

CHARACTER: all characters are voided by her nearness.
her dearness.

DIRECTIONS: stay.

make displacement permanent.

stay.

make light permanent.
and lovingly.
at any reliable angle.
stay or put.
stay or wait.
stay or ride

IT: past another remove, tripping, restlessly aiming.
                    for

IT: this person's turn.
                    that person's turn.
                    run all the turns.
                    then run away in the getaway

VEHICLE: car.

VICTIM: car.

COLOR: car.

SIZE: car.

CAR: didn't ask for this.
                    takes its own sweet.
                    aside and blocks system from operating in its standard
                        erratic manners.
                    encourages a false sense of speed.

CAR: a false sense of timing.

FALSE SECURITY: car.
                    seatbelts everywhere.
                    speed or its lack.
                    rain and its shelter.
                    commitment.
                    reciprocated rain.

water, an interval.

time and its documentation.

ground.

whatever may think itself on it.

FALSE: car.

fast car.

fast words.

fast tender.

descriptions of past events of false or imagined security.

memories of past events where security was implicit or tacitly agreed upon, then aged in a hermetic container as if memory and hermeticism have ever been friends.

friends.

wording of friendship.

declarations of dependence.

avowal and ultimate open.

open as if it is ever safe.

closed books, door.

clothing, warm clothing.

textures such as wool or would.

time such as long length of.

time such as condensed or night or pure

TRUST: pure time.

MISTRUST: time.

FALSE SECURITY: knowing the opposite and every however.

seatbelt on the car-time continuum.

delineating a what-time continuum.
claiming of the person-time continuum.
submitting to the pleasure continuum.
believing in validity.
is pleasure valid.
believing in time.
broken timing belt.
letting go of the need for timing.
believing in pleasure.
is a continuum valid.
is a continuum valid.
or is it safe.
or is it.
if believed enough.
balconics everywhere.

REAL SECURITY: this word at this time in this place to this person.
nothing.
the word, nothing.
the speed of continuance.
the rate at which it passes.
is not secured to any building, architecture, or blue

SPEED: of thought.
of intention.
the speed of no intention moves slower than heavy
    and sounds like nothing no nothing at all.
do we like it.
why speed.
which-speed continuum only goes to follow.

does faster mean truer or is it the reverse.
adverse.
when is truth ever fast.
when is truth ever safe.
speed of safety, if at all.
as opposed to some opinions regarding why any of it.
adversify.
and then dangerously slow.
slow in the false of danger.
going for good

TIME: speeding with supposed necessity.
necessary to leash.
out of the sudden.

DIRECTIONS: 160 cm from the cobble.
continue each day without hedge.

DIRECTION: get off here or get off.

PLACE: in love.
marked by.
water, the next stop.
getting off here.

CHARACTER: unfinanced and turning lovely.
no smudge of security.
owner of the answer.
accepted to institute a practice of this.
hangs above and below, time continuum.

VARIATION: all this with a drink in hand.
              wasted hand clutching a fuzzy memory.
              clutching whose belly.

DIRECTIONS: take heat from one belly to the next.
              take train from one person to the next.
              stand her head upside the platform.
              do it with love.
              do everything with.
              an illusion of security for whatever fraction of each moment.
              spin her eyes to the 47-degree play.
              train her ear to this fashionable train.
              get in

CHARACTER: countable on one digit.
              owner of the voice on the machine.

DIRECTIONS: what is a favor in the all of the above context.
              slightly flat and all the wrong color.
              get it.
              do it.
              ask nicely.
              get in.

DIRECTIONS: feign nicety.
              join up the corners of her mouth.
              keep her at bay.
              water, an interference.
              an illusion of timing.
              dig for goal.

CHARACTER: in relation to a desire towards 2.8 children speaking
                    2.3 languages.
                no trace of an accent.
                an implied right

NOW: all desires and their relationships to all moments coincide
                completely in this particular time and place and never
                anywhere else, as witnessed by all subsequent

CHARACTERS: unwilling to know it.

CHARACTER: built in the style of.
                gender to be determined.
                kindly, the curve of a building.

CHARACTER: historical.

CHARACTER: familiar.

CHARACTER: falls down at the feet of a passing young woman.
                a drunkard.
                a veteran.
                crippled with destitute promises.
                all of them akimbo.

DIRECTIONS: all through the night.
                revived and unusual.
                keep this true and mute the pitch.
                any pitch.

DIRECTIONS: say anything just not what is allowed.
               don't listen to what is said.
               take directions from this voice.
               take directions from not this voice.
               take directions to the limitless

LIMIT: definitive

DEFINITION: of a perceived right.
               a sharpened right.
               perception of right.
               deceptive right.
               legitimate right.

LEGITIMATED: by who.

WHO: mother.
               owner of the answering machine.
               oh

VARIATION: scientific method as re-appropriated by

WHO: persons of motherly interests.
               a dear

PLACE: diffident that way.
               missing a digit, a chance.
               missing an x.

VARIATION: mother, as in central standard.
             water, an interruption.
             mother, as in american wet standard blank

ETIQUETTE: sucks nicety.

TIME: to ask the father.
             conspired against contrition.
             an inspired

TIME: fallen.
             running.
             other dangers called

TIME: quickened or encroaching

TIME: have designs on.
               be still my.
               that was the worst

WORST: a case of scenarios.

CHARACTER: under the bar.
               under the table.
               the sink.

WORST: name for a drink.
               potential to fatten.
               fat collar job.

CASE: hell out of dodginess.

DIRECTIONS: ad.
               sub.
               submit.
               enter.
               wait.
               pick.
               up.
               the call and go to a meeting.
               attend with full uniform of coffee and sugar.
               reflect on the possibility of increase.
               projected potential incoming food. not food.
               money. ask for money.

what is received in this event.
buy her up. buy long. sell

CHARACTER: the same and the growing.
same and the restless.
developmental hard-knocks.

DIRECTIONS: hurt pride.
acute and sharpening.
drop that sucker.
take it south.
park it.
do it better this time.

PLACE: never would have guessed this

PLACE: recurring.
feels like.
falls in love here at almost every 4pm.
falls in love at every long hour.

PLACE: the end of a line.
goes long.
misinterpreted claim.

PLACE: for a good hang-up.

PLACE: for a recurring illusion.

PLACE: it.

HERE: now.

AGAIN: nothing.

AGAIN: same old nothing.
                   self-made nothing.

PLACE: a sand.
                   a south sand.
                   scraping together a sentiment.
                   upon scrapping a tour of.
                   under left arm of.
                   someone's long neck

PLACEMENT: try it for size or shape.
                   in the mouth.
                   of all

TIMES: had by all.
                   having been marred

TIME: to trip intuit.

TIME: having been dessert, inserted sweet gesture of

ANOTHER TIME: to receive another reconciliation

TIME: to take the cotton.
                   and sweeten or.
                   run.
                   in

FIRST: two-ring floor plan.
                     candied, childed, and left behind

DIRECTIONS: laugh out extra time.
                     to the tea.
                     ceremonious or commencing at the dot.
                     progressing into a line.
                     aligned love.

SECOND: ring.
                     blown out.
                     minutiae or minutely.
                     had it had it minutely.
                     third love.
                     as

SECOND PLACE: vixed nor longing.
                     white boat or white hat.
                     elongated train.
                     to the farthest attention.

RING: to the farthest mouth.
                     militiae or minutes of.
                     finger.
                     meeting

ROOM: unfillable box.

DIRECTIONS: open at dusk.

ENTER: a door in.
              to the outduskish and light of it.
              caught a dune.

DUNE: momentile expansion.
              vixed and asked of it.
              momentile expulsion.

WAIT: another or moment.

WAITED: for direction.

WAITING: forward.
              for a clenched anonymous

GOD: fast forward.
              as in oh.

GO: back to a cow.

COW: for cooked meat.
              exampled insecurity.
              mouth full of moo.
              negligible insertion.
              money in the mouth.
              have one

MOUTH: look up or north.
              bigger or farther.
              or father.

or fisher.

or mistaken for a man.

or found used and dumb.

or found golden difference.

or found opening tenuous, mouth slowly heading north in a desperate search for light and lighter, mouth slowly heading light along a vagrant fence, mouth slowly ignoring guards, border drawn in ocean, mouth forming a group of willing people, help, assistance, at times not to be trusted, mouth faltering its own roots, mouth formulating tender hopes and a thickness of such, mouth templating a thickness, a path one could follow, mouth thickening of its own founded hopes and its own founded youths and haves and children to cross it up, mouth crossing it up, a terrible suburban, three mouths hold hands and cross the freeway, mouth darkens mouth lightens mouth holds tight speeding to the north the north and an entry.

and what
and in what

TIME: minus 20.

minus the space between you and your own left foot, the foot which left.

minus the moisture.

minus the hand.

minus the second.

minus the second hand as a moment to sleep.

minus catching a slip.

minus stride, not quickening, lengthening, progressing
   or nor.
minus element.
minus a twentieth beginning.
minus first one to.
minus the addition.
minus more to come, more relative.
minus trying again having been trying it again minus
   tracting or traction, minus the left behind

CHARACTER: statistical cretins.

MINUS: versus.
   or again.
   organs.

AGAIN: timing as out to get us.

TIME: mind us.
   or.
   mouth agape.

CHARACTERS: language mouth.
   brother mouth.
   round of an intellectual

MOUTH: falters away.
   fades to a close.
   gets up early to take off.
   an innocent.

back to a downy.
the owner of

DIRECTIONS: large or wider farther left.
go back and righten it up.
flop into a fake chair.
slip in underneath, bite of tongue.
meet me any time at the right place.

TIME: on a busted watch.
busted up geography.
a timely breakage.
to ask for a hand.
in.
or

DO: pleased to be extenuous hand.
how do you

KNOW: what to get religious about.
what to hold on to.
where the tangible ends up

WHERE: the crooked people go.
the good stuff is kept.
the keeper goes to take a break.

BREAK: cathedrals everywhere.
praying moments everywhere.
incestuous relations

WHERE: basement.
corridor.
balcony.
unshoveled sidewalk.
in the nest of her head.
space between two palms.
flatness of silence.
where there was supposed to be laughter.

BREAK: missed intentions.
missed mates.
missed phone call.
ringing everywhere but

HERE: hallway.

HERE: aisle inside a mind.

HERE: island on which moon.
breaking everywhere.

HERE: back up against transit time.
everywhere running over

DROPPING: bombs of color.
bottoms.
bursting with

AIR: a heart full of.
head full of.

cocked but not ready.
dropped and shot

DROPPING: mid-flight.
postcards.
the fly-over states.

WATER: minnesota.
michigan.
chicago.
the kitchen sink.
a bath.
crying in the shower.
crying everywhere.
bathing everywhere.
in the wrong

LIGHT: always a right place for.

WRONG: cactus light.
a drink lightened in color.
smile lightened with time.
wrinkles lightened with surgery.

NOT WRONG: wrinkles in time.

WRONG: turning the other face.
the other turn.
not taking the turn.
facing up too late.

RIGHT: at the nearest corner.
under this table.
away, this is my first.
or chronologic.
break to the nearest.
or dialogic.
breaking it up.
or altered logic.
dirty logic.

HIT: dirt.
drop.
semi-darkness at a sharp angle.
hit motion, a

STOP: caution

STOP: familiar

STOP: in front of the right house.

RIGHT: at the wrong house.

RIGHT: in front of a distant memory of.
bad sex.
bad bad sex.

STOP: there.

STOP: breaks in the streetlight.
feels a trap.
springs.
top of her anxious.
boxed in

VOICE: prowling this way.

VOICE: riding it out till dawnbreak.
shaken and piggybacked.
wrongly flirted.
wringing.
and ringing

VOICE: cheating a crack.
beckons.
bleak

FACE: sharp cheekbones.

NOSE: tied up.

EYES: pointed and outbound.
listening or panting.
linking and a scan.

MOUTH: breaking that way.
open for the longest.
empty slot, empty slot.
right out the back door.

CALLING: back the mouth, eyes, face.

WAITING: for the eyeline to arrive.

ASKING: for a new arrangement.

GETTING: the same distanced look.
feigned and nicety.
or worse, wrong nicety.

WANTING: another eye.

BREATHING: in, it all in.
a newer injunction.
half-melted, bitterness.
hard to swallow.
hard to digest.
hard to wrap the body around

BREATH: can't hear it.
can't feel it.
can't see it.

and when it is seen, felt, heard, smelled.
and when it is smelled.
and when it is smelled, accompanied.

ACCOMPLICE: silently waiting for you.
for sale on the street.
a threadbare pointless line.

POINTLESS LINE: nothing to hang onto.
                  from.
                  to shining

ACCOMPLICE: a restless situation.

WITNESS: a hapless situation.
                  suspicious of time.

CRIMINAL: helping out in times of

NEED: two pairs of recently sharpened scissors.
                  two recently sharpened minds.
                  two somnambulists.
                  two functional minds.
                  two funky minds.
                  two best.
                  two yous.
                  a use.

FULL OF: heart.
                  a tender knot.
                  stomach.
                  a warm wound.
                  needless fuss.
                  pee.
                  outlandish gestures of grandeur.
                  mouth.
                  desolation.
                  heat.

                      all of it.
                      all of it.
                      all of it.

ABOVE: yes.

BELOW: yes.

CENTER: all of it.

RIGHT SIDE: all flying and breaking.

LEFT SIDE: out.

EYE LEVEL: is 25 degrees higher than actual

CHEST LEVEL: somebody's hard head.
                      a hard ass head.
                      heady ass.

ASS LEVEL: bursting with.
                      run like stink.

STINK: cowshit as owned by a human.
                      new dimensions of bullshit.
                      cutting it all off.
                      with a knife.

TENSION: breaking everywhere.
                      dropping everywhere.
                      is.

or.

as.

broken.

beaten.

given.

left.

thickened.

stewed.

pounded.

driven.

onto everybody's backs.

BACK LEVEL: swimming out of a paper bag.

floating unpeacefully.

treading.

treading.

treading.

treading.

TREND: to drive fast.

eat well.

drink up.

go out.

to appear.

appear.

to appear all of the above.

all of the below.

to appear well.

all of the upper.

to appear as.

all of the best.
to appear as opposed to believe. not belie.
to appear to have conviction. to have to appear convinced.
to have nothing we mean nothing but conviction.
really.

REAL: roasted.
         gross.
         original.

REAL: meat.
         connection.
         spiced with a loaded up and

JUICY: stories about fruitcakes.
         stories about trendy people.
         stories about real people.
         stories about other people.
         stories having nothing to do.
         stories having much to do.
         stories having everything to do,
         all of the above appearing.
         as if real.
         all of it as if real.

REAL: and real.

REAL: this is real.

REAL: this is reality.

REAL: this is really reality.

REAL: breaking everywhere.
           news.
           of the.

REAL: belonging to it.
           possessing it.
           possessing a clue.
           belonging with it.
           belonging together.
           belonging to this reality as opposed to which other reality.
           flying all over the place.
           driving all over the place.
           driving us all out of our chairs.
           a real chair.
           a real drive.
           out to the countryside.
           out of the real city.
           critical real city.
           critical real mass city.

MASS: of a real city.
           at a real city.
           real mass of a city.
           breaking everywhere.
           ask the cathedrals.

ASK: the city.
           the dislocated city.

the displaced city.
where is your shoulder.
where is your mother.
where is your home, you little.

ASK: the mother, as in oh.
the scientist, cultural.
questions in the form of answers.

ASK: in standardized questions.
in increasing increments of three.
in turn asking for a favorite.
in turn asking for a spot.
whoever remains standing.
to be caught and held dancing.
mothers dancing everywhere.

ASK: mothers to stop dancing.
the reasons for mothers dancing.
mothers as dancers.
mothers then dancers.
mothers become dancers.

DANCERS: breaking everywhere.
make bodily cathedrals.
make everywhere.
do everywhere.
everywhere via the body.
dance everywhere.
and fall.

and turn.
and spiral everywhere,
this is a multi-direction.
a daily regimen.
daily look in the mirror.
sustenance or sustained by.
music, sustenance of
rhythm, sustenance of
timing.
time.
sustenance of a better time.
sustenance of waiting time.
sustained wait.
suspended wait.
waiting to fall.
waiting to drop.
waiting to cause the fall.
fall instigators.
drop instigators.
floor instigators.
moving a wall instigators.
dancing away instigators.
falling away instigators.
following it in instigators.
thank you for instigations.
thank you for dancing this way.
thank you for dancing in an exit.
thank you you've moved a wall.

WALL: thanks you.
            takes you.
            holds you.
            up.
            up.

UP: holding a wall.

MEANT: to be contained.
            to be containable.
            to be embracing amidst the trampled outside.

UP: directional tenderness.
            noncommittally going there.
            quantum scooping upwards.

SCOOP: all reality is really below.

HER BELOW: opened to false security.
            embraces the trampled outside.

BELOW HER: a pent-up loud voice.
            a need you to not.
            knotted decisions.
            tangle you.
            leave you at the beeline.
            leave you period.
            leave you this is a break.
            leave you wandering.
            leave you at the blue.

leave you at the blue line.

took too long.

leave you at a blue pitch.

pitched and blue.

leave you stalled.

leave you unsharpened.

floored.

leave you in an altered state.

without a motive.

unmatched.

leave you stuffed.

unwieldy, off-balance.

fall into a trap.

stumble through the fall.

mess up the fall.

failed drop.

net total.

adding up the negative space.

adding up the leavings.

leavenings.

risings.

from the dredge.

leave you up.

texturings.

texture of a motive.

leave you below.

with or without the negative space.

with and without the negative space.

leave you off.

with side without side which side.

to leave you.
to leaven and leaven.
with floor as leverage.
with bread as leverage.
with flat bread.
with negative bread.
with bleeding bread.
with blue bread.
left you below with blue bread and will it be just as bad as
leaving you off the line, will it, or will the line take you off
of the blue, taking the blue off of the line but will it still
be still be still be bread.
or blood.

BELOW: an opening mouth.
anopening mouth.
nopening mouth.
nope-nope.

NOPE: transmitted.

NOPE: awaited.

NOPE: encrypted.

NOPE: embracing against the trample.
withheld and smiled upon.
source of the smile.
real of the smile.
a smile called truth.

a smiled called wait.
a smile called still.
a smile called hope you.
a smile called fuck you.
a smile called still.
a smile called sill.
a smile called this window, still, this window, still, you.
a smile called meant to say.
a smile called what do you mean nope.

NOPE: a smile called.
                           dangerous smiles.

THIS SITUATION: calls for a smile.

YOUR SITUATION: calls for a true.

MY SITUATION: calls out for.

FOR: other dangers called

YES: lingering nope.
              opening nope.
              hopping nope.
              hoping nope.
              written nope.
              promised nope.
              it's on, nope, it's on

TOP: or is it surface.
              nope it's surface.
              negation of surface leaves you on

TOP: let out the reality.
              let out the illusion of reality.
              let out a small scoop of reality.
              check below.
              let out a loud voice.
              let out the wall.
              wail.
              no thank you.
              let out a real need you to knot.
              let out a tangle.
              let it all tangle.
              and wail.
              let them sort it out.
              pay dearly for the wedding band.
              see the event clearly.
              surfaces of action.
              face of an actor.
              surfeit, take it out.

smoothing the usual edges.
smoothing the edges of the beeline.
something holding it up to a tee, a period.
something breaking on a dime.
something taking a break.
break in the surface.
a break-in at the surface.
surface marriage.
wandering in through the break in the surface.
waiting in.
wading around on top.
every line of the surface.
the top of the surface, atop it.
smoothenings

ATOP: a colored line.
a coded line.
a code surfacing in line.
a code surfacing in field.
a cold surface in the field.
a field of I want this to be.

TRUE: real.
really atop.
stalled on the surface.

ATOP: stalled on a sharp note.
stalled or getting floored.

ATOP: stalled alone.

ATOP: stalled emotion.
             stalled motive.
             stalled spark.
             the gross total, getting atop it.
             positive space, scrambling.
             and then leaving it.

A REACH: to the trample.

AGAIN: to the good-light.
             the near-light.
             dear-light.
             dear attentive.
             to the nearest attention.
             the weakest light.
             a light removal.
             slight removal.
             light understatement.
             near removal.
             to the broad-light.
             the once-light.
             natural light, as captured in this basket, sold at the light
                 market for quite a misfortune.
             convicted.

AGAIN: the misfortune of light.
             an arguably misfortunate.
             light as a missed fortune.

AGAIN: light as active male principle.
             light as active he-principle.

light as active heat.
to be active as heat.
to be determinate.
be determined.
stay.
to be away.
go.
to lead.
to lend.
to the lent light.
to the advisory light.
to the caution.
to the caustic light.
to the intentional light.

AND: an intentional lightness vs. an actual lightness.
actuality of light.
vacuous light or.

AND: an acting light.
a directed light.
a direct act.
of light.
of imagined lightness.
of created light.
and destroyed.
which is true.

TRUE: and.

AND: true.

            or.

ELSE: a new substance.

            a new definition.

            a new stiffness.

            a new iffiness.

            a new sore.

            a new degeneration of.

            newly confessed.

            newly bewedded.

            newly beheaded.

            a new light.

            sentenced to.

NEW: time.

            place.

            directions.

            characters.

            character.

            person.

            directive.

            timing.

            placement.

            variation.

            note.

            pitch.

            timbre.

            muse.

            color.

character.
hands.
hands in transit.
hands for cathedrals.
collapsing.
clapping in on.
sound.
solidification.
set.
mold.
molded bread.
colored bread.
setting.
plot.
stage.
offstage.
a new offstage.
theme.
a bad recurring theme.
a bad kid.
bad kid in everyone.
bad theme bad theme.
irony.
bad themes everywhere.
bad times everywhere.
bad irony is bad.

NEW: show of irony.
              costume.

makeup.
revolutionary ideas about kissing.
resolutionary notions about kissing.
climax.

NEW: leading questions.
spoken sex.
sailing sex.
continuous sex.
tension sex.
false sex.

NEW: dropped sex.
dropped phone.
dropped phone sex or angry.
dropped triangle.
sex with a dog.
sex with humans.
sex with parents.
angry droppings all over the street.
they are not

NEW: conflict.
new conflict.
new conflict.
now this is not

NEW: blanks.
blanket filler material.

new train ride full of material.
new train ride full of prayer.
new train ride is not at all

NEW: plot.
          of a conflict filled with sex.
          filled with character.
          fill her up with character.

BUILD: a new building.
          with more character.

NEW: plot of tenuous land.
          plot over several years.
          resistance over several years.
          time to resist.
          time to eat.
          time to engage.

NEW: newly engaged proof of dementia.

NEW: newly qualified cathedrals.

NEW: newly bewildered lovers who.
          don't even know it.

NEW: newly specified lightness.
          barflies who think they can fly.
          the weight of our collaborative lies.

NEW: newly assigned directions.
        smatterings of hope.
        good old shatter.

NEW: same newness comes back to haunt.

NEW: newly victimized under the influence of.
        newness.

NEW: or false.
        and false.
        as security.
        at eye level.

TALL: asking for it.
        didn't order this.
        drink with a fly in it.
        to fly in it.
        eat this you

READ: really.
        mean this you

MEANT: to be honest, sincere, and good yes good.
        good no good.
        that good or this good.
        to start stopping to suffer.
        good this you

WANTED: to be real.
            to be true.
            to be true.
            to be truth.

MEANT: forget it you

MEANT: to be other.
            to not be tyrannical.
            to be free from at least its own tyranny.
            to be upper limit.
            up the ante.
            meant it up the ante.

MEANT: to fill it up.
            her heart full of gas.
            gasoline.
            glycerine.
            blank heart.
            light heart.
            light heat.
            blanket her heart with.
            this you

MEANT: this to be.
            us to be.
            it to be.

MEANT: it all to be.
            taken, for you
            had given, for you

MEANT:	it to be taken for stone or granite, to be lasting and wearing and precious and wet, a parkled warm laughter over this and any which distance, distance slipping, meant to be slippable and carried in this eye's ear, visual ear, see it, meant to be I see, meant to be I hear, meant to be carrying or continuing in the ear, long after all
EYES:	on hand.
EYES:	on hand meant to be ear meant to be heard.
EYES:	on it meant to be warm.
WARM:	meant to be giving.
WARM:	meant to be chosen.
	meant to be filling.
	meant to be captured with pleasure.
	meant to be balanced.
	meant to be knee.
	meant to be cheek.
	kissy.
	meant to be arms.
	meant to be covered up, warm, cool, fitting, exterior.
OUT:	meant to be open.
	meant to be heard open and heard seeing and heard long, long after, meant to be still true.
NEW:	directions for entry.

DIRECTIONS: new.

NEW: directions for false entry.
              brave new seemingly innocuous threshold.
              border.
              hyper-extended family.
              back door to the lobby.
              front door.
              welcome mat.
              floor mat.
              foot mat.
              dirt mat.
              shower mat.
              shit mat.
              dog mat.
              hair mat.
              sick mat.
              unwelcome mat.
              unwelcome mat.

DIRECTIONS: at not here.

DIRECTIONS: at not there.

DIRECTIONS: at anyone but.
              everyone not.
              unsuspecting directives.

CHARACTER: arrive on top of the time.

CHARACTER: follow many directions.
            follow too many directions.
            follow the wrong directions for a lot of money.
            follow it out.

CHARACTERS: one door.
             one geography.
             young french intellect, hard.
             old mexican intellect, stiffed.
             one window flying.
             one dying.
             an open.
             one tenderness dying.
             an out.
             one tenuous flying.
             brink of flying.
             sinking down a width of air.
             sinking towards a surfeit of water.
             crossing a liquid border.
             bad fluidity.
             liquefied friendship.
             one spectator.
             one witness.
             one incidental.
             an accidental.
             one mother.
             one oh.
             negotiates between any characters from below.
             negotiates between any matter.
             or her heart, full of

IT: asked for over the course of several birthdays.
            asked for in every language.

IT: given with hundreds of strings.

IT: noted to self.
            dropped

IT: on.
            fish butcher's head.
            mouth full of salt.
            tongue full of ch'i.

IT: innocently.
            aghastly.
            unbelievably.
            childlessly.
            wonderlessly.

IT: meant to be it.
            letting them know about

IT: wanting to come on

IT: every tomorrow night.
            tapping it in, or fill

IT: with the best person.
            with the current best person.
            with the probable currently best person.

with the somewhat probably best person.
with the more than somewhat

IT: like they always said.
          never delivered.
          or on

TIME: it.

TIME: dead.

TIME: end.

TIME: when to return to when.

TIME: for apologies.
          to a rock.
          a person.
          mineral.
          missing person.
          to a lost person.
          a stringy person.

PERSON: outside of his natural environment.

NATURAL: as corn.
          an ear.
          a whiff of sex on a passing intellect.

NATURAL: passing too swiftly for the catching.

CAUGHT: another whiff.
another passing intuition.
another country to cross.
another train to throw.
another sentimental moon.
deconstructed cow.
piece of steak, for the

FIRE: this burning burning

FIRE: feeling outside

FIRE: mother, if not oh

FIRE: no escape from

TIME: immemorial.

ESCAPE: if only the security were truly false.
if only the butcher, true to his knife.
if only the tenuous would.
the tenuous would announce itself.
fish itself out.
of its own fires.
its own breakage.
breaking point as truly happening or truly approaching.
about to happen as real.
about to happen as not quite yet real.
about to happen as on the brink of falsity.
about to go false.

bulbous.
with an unpleasant smell.

BAD: escape tactics.
escape dreams.
whiffs of escape.
whiffs of embrace.
whiffs of affection, as in a missed hug.
good huggy intentions.

GOOD: goo.
rid.

BAD: is it good.
is it real.
is it mugged.
is it secure to be good.
the innocence of characters.
that's so.

AND SO: extended goodness.
a kind mouth.

AND SO: a kind of mouth.

AND SO: good, as returned in the form of a mouth, tenuously
      held open.
bad, offered up as a mouthful.
an opening, for good.
a cleave, for the common.

cure for the common cleave.
not this

TIME: once referred to as a wrinkle.
as cleft.
as cold.
riddance.
itch of someone's skin.
about to go long.

TIME: automated hunger.
casual hunger develops into something worse.

ELAPSED TIME: while forcing laughter.
forging laughter.
false duration.
laughter automatic.

TIME: standing in for.
batting for.
going in for.
in for

NOT IT: meant to be.
meant to be what.
meant to be one

TENDENCY: one.
for starters.
towards light.

towards imagined light.
towards fading light.
towards hoar.
to war

TIME: to kill.
          still itching

TIME: looking upon languor from a distance.
          looking pensive from a distance.
          looking extensively at the distance.
          tensive.
          in

TIME: on it.
          on it.
          on

SUSPENSION: suspect to removal or.
               hunger gets refracted into

BREAK:

in.

TIME: just.
         perfect.
         syncopated

TIME: scientific negation of

TIME: integral to

BREAK: a long promise.
            cracked windshield expanding.
            hard on the line.
            envelope, pushing a new

EDGE: becomes corner.
            becoming.
            woman.
            corner of a woman.
            becoming order.
            mature audience.
            falls prey to, or ripened

EDGE: of two bodies.
            torque.
            glass on mouth.
            ice, water, or glass

MOTIVE: to continue a slow recede.
            to constitute a downpour.
            to continue in a weak light.
            to constitute a meltdown.
            to count out the usual.
            to count on a new break.

SUSPECT: time.

SUSPECT: overtime.

SUSPECT: belief.

WORSE: conviction.

SUSPECT: rampant imbecile.

HOLD: tongues.
                hostage at the speakeasy.

HOLD: on a look.
                on a clension.
                on a black box.
                on another balk.
                of declension.
                of real.
                of late.

HOLD: on a mast.
                on a wind.
                on it rolling around inside a tight space of mouth.
                on it on hands with a clutch.
                on it on lips.
                curled around the corner digging, digging it.

HOLD: inside the eyes a clean burn.

OUT: hold it or send it.
                toeing it.
                someone were to take it.
                knowing when to take it.
                a line inside the store, only waiting to get

OUT: having a place to take it.

having time to take place.

having time over

AND AT: a lack of communicable.

a friendly distance.

friends as disease.

not

FRIENDS: ailments,

NOT: nourishing.

friendships.

NOT: your father's oh.

brother, as in my.

NOT: asking for it again.

NOT: gaining.

gaining on.

NOT: lost time.

having time to lose.

having time in the first place.

having ever been in the first place.

in the first place.

in first place.

NOT: the man in first place.
            the woman in first place.

NOT: the first man.
            the first woman.
            first woman to get

NOTHING: but first love.

NOTHING: on the balcony but.
            impulsive droppings from.
            impulsive fallings from.
            impulsive falls in.
            let's take a photograph.
            says

NO ONE: but all of it.
            but all of this.
            but all of the airspace breathspace dreamspace heldspace
            armspace legroom nightspace seaspace soundspace glow-
            space lightspace thinspace skyspace dropspace jump-
            space glasspace passpace ifspace whenspace safespace
            safespace safespace kindspace freespace if only for a lone
            if only for a thispace borrowed moment and then to have
            none of it or all over

IT: looking for

IT: wanting for

IT: hoping for

IT: having had.
         having had this.
         having been given.
         having been complected.
         having been lovely.
         having been loving.
         having been love.
         having been I want.
         having been all good fortunate lines of reception.
         line.
         having been in line.
         been on it.
         having been lied to.
         having been the line underfoot.
         having been one step on the off-chance, one step on
         the line underfoot, one step on a balcony, one step on a
         tight line of joy, one step on a solid stream of light, one
         step wobbling upon the approaching tenuous, one step
         mired in a past conviction, one step gone dark and lovely,
         one step upon an interjection, a line of thought, one step
         up on

IT: had having.
         had giving.
         had a practiced give.
         yielding or giving.
         had character.
         had direction.

had time.

plenty.

had subject.

subjectivity.

had suspect.

vulnerability.

everywhere.

had fissure.

anywhere.

had plot.

lot.

multiplying plot.

had cheek.

many.

and tongues.

checked.

had the kindest sides.

had the warmest distance.

had the tender.

tend her.

had a letter.

had many.

had many physical letters of increasing occasion.

had birthdays.

had other birthdays.

had other people's breakups.

had lengthened occasions.

had multiple repeat occasions.

to cry.

crying everywhere.

cathedrals everywhere.
no religion.
belief everywhere.
but.
but.
unconvincing arguments anywhere, but

IT: had every argument.
had every refusal.
had every personal.
had one step on every stake.
had one stake in every heart.
one take.
one taken.
one heart speeding away.
on a plane.
driven like a car.
heat dropping everywhere heat

IT: heard.
almost heard.
wanted to be heard.
wanted to be heard still.
was hers in the first place.
heard out.
never heard out.
encrypted.
jammed.
written and not heard.
written or heard.

or not written.
or not said.
neither here nor hurt.
and all over

IT: as all over.
as game over.
as sleep over.
as left over.
as all over the place.
what is heard.
what was given.
what was gifted.
what was shining, trilled and forthright, what was left with or what

was remaindered or what was sustained, haunted, residing, residual, what was suspended, revoked, reinvited, then expelled, removed, anulled, forged, thrown out on the next line, received from the next line, explained in the same line, not understanding, not standing, not liking being under, under it, under a large overhead heave, wreckage, not wanting to get caught, caught under it, nor wanting to catch it, never having thrown it, thrown out, who threw what out, like trash, furniture, like a dog, who threw out what, what, what this means, what this means, where this meant,

IT: what it never meant to be.
                  what it tightly tried to mean.
                  what it hoped it would never mean

IT: to stand behind it.
                  to go to bat for it.
                  to move out for it.
                  to move in for it.
                  to lay it on its own line.
                  to lay everything on its own line.
                  to lay down the line.
                  to lay down a thick line.
                  what this means.
                  to have thickened.

what this meant.
to have crossed.
jumped.
stepped over.
driven over.
flown over.
the line.
small line with no hope for measurement.
thick line with no hope for erasure.

DRAWN: in desperate times.
in desperation for measurement.
in asking for measurable forward progress.
progress of any sort.
sort of progress.
sortable progress.
to stop regressing.
to stop regretting.
to stop

IT: a let-go.
secret car.
walk in the park.
not so easy as.
walking apart.
not so easy as.
driving fast.
endless returns.
easy case of illness.
difficult case of sleep.

approaching a landing.
difficult line of sleep.
or thought.
difficult length of sleep.
plotting to sleep it off.
shake it off.
rub it off.
travel it off.
train it off.
drive it off.
eat it off.
drink it off.
move it off.
move it.
off-subject.
off-topic.
off of her most sensitive parts and onto the

TABLE: point of view.
late arrival.
substitute.
a kind woman who enters and opens windows.
keeps opening windows.
until they fly open.
their own accord.
fly off.
everyone trying to shake it off.
sound of all the windows.
sound of shaking it off.
everything.

what this meant.
bordering on meaning.
minimalistically.
pragmatically.
logically.
selfishly.
shyly.
boldly.
nicely nicely.
not

THIS: time.

NOT: again.

NOT: in the nearest future.

NOT: desirable outcomes.
           desirable outbound flights to a foreign country where all
                language is missing, different, or safely stowed away.

NOT: stowed anywhere.

NOT: owed to anyone.

NOT: it.
           ends up being

NOT: for a short time.
           or long period.

which this meant.
what this never meant to be

AND: tenuous on its own terms.
tenuous insofar as it believes itself to be.
tenuous measure of distance.
tenuous act of sincerity

AND: tenuous end of a line.
tenuous word hanging midair.
tenuous trying desperately to ground itself.
tenuous seduced by the lovely and the magical

AND: tenuous daring to reach.
tenuous asking for another chance.
tenuous asking for yet another.
tenuous asking for what should have been the last time

AND: tenuous hanging on and on to the last time the last line.
tenuous groping for a better word.
tenuous noting, keeping, guarding this moment.
tenuous taking it all in as a pain, pleasure, gift

AND: tenuous nose for disaster.
tenuous head in disaster.
tenuous headed for disaster.
tenuous coming to terms with disaster.
letting go of its own terms

AND: tenuous redefining.
         tenuous redefining its terms and for whom.
         tenuous reaching out for another gift of time, illusions
              of timing.
         tenuous adding up the time, filling in blanks, claiming
              ownership,
         tenuous claiming to be somewhere, own something,
              have stakes, be at stake

OR: tenuously searching for ground

AND: tenuous place called partially.
         tenuous person, somewhere, who likes it.
         tenuous and covered over, cloaked, a winter coat,
              malicious words, glares, silences,
         tenuous holding its tongue.

AND: tenuous declaring its true intentions in silence with
              a stance in silence.
         tenuous turn and turning, the options.
         tenuous returning to a nebulous desire.

AND: tenuous making a phone call.
         tenuous writing down words.
         tenuous handing them over.
         handing them over.
         tenuous speaking and to whom.

AND: tenuous letting go.
         tenuous letting.
         tenuous going.

                    tenuous leaving.

AND: all of the below.

BELOW: light.
                    light in memorial.
                    lighter for a cigarette.
                    lighter in a darker place.
                    the dark place.

AND BELOW: memory wins out.

RATHER: no winners.
                    no wind of.
                    no talk left.
                    and everything

SUCH AS: time.
                    directions.
                    characters.
                    moving characters.
                    interchangeable characters.
                    intervening characters.
                    intersecting characters.
                    interloping characters.
                    interested characters.
                    invested characters.
                    inviting characters.
                    all go out for a drink.
                    for a fuck.
                    all go out of this

STORY: ending.
poetry.
game.
play.
all go out of this.

ALL: going everywhere.

ALL: going somewhere.
asking the bartender for another place to go.
asking the bar for another line of music.

ALL: asking to be kindred.
asking to be a kinder voice.
a better extrication.
exit stragedy.

ALL: voices on the phone.
remainders of voice.

SOME: remains of surgery.
remains of sex.
remains of believing.
of idiocy.
of trusting.

REMAINS: of all of it, some anywhere.
of none except for what is spoken.

ALL: of what was never spoken.
of what was always meant.

                          still meant.
                          still carrying meaning.

ALL: intentions everlasting.

ALL: intentional goings-away.

ALL: travel for the sake of others.
                          remainders of movement, displacement, transport.
                          geography of risk.

SOME: internal topography.
                          measurement of

TIME: for an enormous

TIME: for an unusual

TIME: breaking anywhere.

My sincere thanks go out first to my parents and my brother. And then to Sally Picciotto, Barbara Carra, Bobbie West, Françoise Choquet, Vijaya Jhothi, Don Kish, Diana Peattie, Cole Heinowitz, and John Granger, for their friendship, kindness, and general goofiness. To Suzanne Torres and Shoshana Michael, wherever you are. To the following writers I am grateful for their inspiration and encouragement, and for reading various drafts of this book: Kerri Sonnenberg, Anna Joy Springer, Forrest Gander, Sandy Florian, Carole Maso, Thalia Field, Mark Tardi, Ruth Margraff, John Lowther, Stacia Saint Owens, Keith and Rosmarie Waldrop, and Craig Watson. And finally, thanks to the following editors for printing excerpts from this book in their journals: Tracy Grinnell at Aufgabe, *Sue Landers at* Pom-Pom, *and Laura Solomon at* Castagraf.

In one sense this book is for those people who have given me their time and love. In a particular sense this book is for Chris, for giving me his time and love.

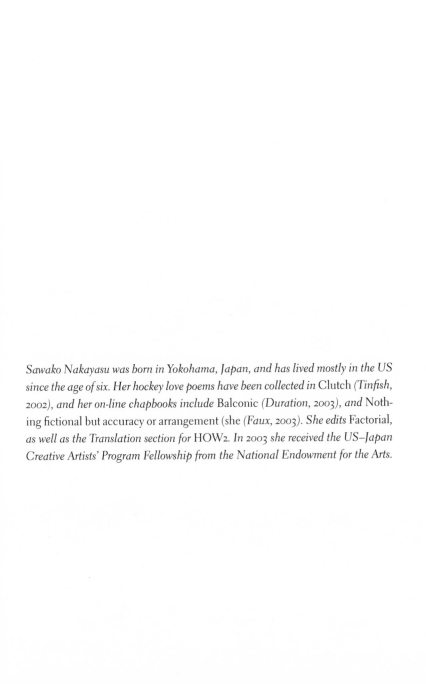

Sawako Nakayasu was born in Yokohama, Japan, and has lived mostly in the US since the age of six. Her hockey love poems have been collected in Clutch *(Tinfish, 2002), and her on-line chapbooks include* Balconic *(Duration, 2003), and* Nothing fictional but accuracy or arrangement (she *(Faux, 2003). She edits* Factorial, *as well as the Translation section for HOW2. In 2003 she received the US–Japan Creative Artists' Program Fellowship from the National Endowment for the Arts.*